Introduction

Environmental issues are often in the news – climate change, pollution and sustainability are typical examples. These issues can seem remote from our daily lives, even though it is our everyday actions at work, home and leisure that can cause global environmental problems which can, in turn, have a major effect on our health, home, local surroundings and way of life. As individuals we are all responsible for the environment and it is now commonly recognised that even apparently insignificant individual actions can result in significant beneficial changes to the en

Chapter 1
Environmental impacts and sustainability

Defining the environment

The environment can be defined simply as 'the conditions or circumstances of living' or, as in the Environmental Management Systems Standard ISO 14001, as the 'surroundings in which an organisation operates, including air, water, land, natural resources, flora, fauna, humans and their interrelation.'

There are five key environmental issues that affect us all:

- resource depletion
- pollution (air, water and land)
- climate change
- loss of biodiversity
- statutory nuisances.

Resource depletion

The Earth has a finite set of resources that support our way of life — they include:

- gas, oil and coal to provide power and heating

- water, soil, plants and animals to provide food

- minerals and trees to provide building materials to help shelter us from the elements.

Resource depletion occurs when natural resources are used at a higher rate than they can be replenished.

Resource depletion is caused by:

- population growth

- inefficient planning and use of resources.

To prevent resource depletion, governments are introducing measures to:

- use resources more efficiently

- use renewable sources of energy (wind, wave and solar) instead of non-renewable sources (carbon-based coal and oil)

- recycle waste.

Pollution

Pollution is the release of substances that cause harm to:

- humans – for instance poisoning, asthma and cancers

- property – for instance structural damage to buildings

- the environment – for instance poisoning and loss of habitat and food sources.

6 Environmental Principles and Best Practice

Air pollution

Air pollution causes a number of serious problems including:

- poor air quality

- depletion of the ozone layer

- acid rain.

Poor air quality can result in ill health – for example respiratory conditions.

The ozone layer:

- is a naturally occurring layer of gas, positioned 15–25 miles up in the Earth's stratosphere

- protects the Earth's surface from harmful ultra violet (UV) rays

- is continually being broken down and reformed naturally.

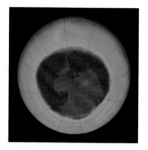

CFCs have caused the
ozone layer to thin

Acid rain damages
the environment

The 'hole' in the ozone layer – a decrease of stratospheric ozone –
was first reported in 1974 and linked to the increasing presence of a
class of man-made compounds called chlorofluorocarbons (CFCs).

Since a worldwide agreement to phase out ozone-depleting
substances (ODS) came into force in 1989, the thinned area in the
ozone layer has stopped getting bigger and may close over the
Antarctic by 2050.

The fight to save the ozone layer is a rare environmental success
story and demonstrates that concerted international action can
provide the opportunity for the environment to repair itself.

Acid rain is formed when gases emitted in the burning of fossil fuels
react in the atmosphere to create harmful acidic precipitation.
Acid rain has harmful effects on surface water and aquatic life,
soil, trees and other plants, and can cause damage to buildings.

Noise and light pollution, particularly in cities, is a cause of illness and stress in human populations.

Water pollution

Clean water is vital to humans, animals and plants. Water pollution usually comes from:

- domestic waste, from dishwashing and toilets
- effluent from industrial processes
- agricultural waste.

Water pollution can affect:

- surface water – seas, rivers, streams and lakes
- groundwater (water held in natural rock formations beneath the Earth's surface)

People who drink contaminated water or eat food that has been in contact with contaminated water while growing or during preparation are at risk of contracting diseases, some of which maybe life-threatening.

Polluted water may also poison and kill aquatic plants and animals.

Water pollution comes
from domestic waste

and agricultural waste

Water pollution can
affect rivers, streams
and lakes

and the sea

Land pollution

Land pollution occurs when an area of land contains a substance that may cause harm to humans, wildlife or property. The main sources of land pollution include:

- old industrial sites

- abandoned mines and quarries

Land pollution can have a number of harmful effects, including:

- human injury and ill health resulting from direct contact with a pollutant or contamination of the water supply or through crop absorption of pollutants

- harm and death to wildlife

- fires or explosions caused by dangerous gases or materials

- damage to buildings caused by pollutants, such as oil and coal tars, which can damage plastic pipes and building materials.

Flytipping can result in land pollution

Land pollution can cause harm to humans, wildlife and property

Climate change

Climate change describes the rise in mean global temperature caused by the release of heat-trapping gases.

Loss of biodiversity

Biodiversity describes the number and variety of animal and plant species on Earth. Human life depends on diversity within ecosystems, both within and between species.

An ecosystem can be described as the interlinking relationship between animals and plants and their environment in a defined area – small (e.g. a garden pond) or large (e.g. a desert).

A rise in the mean global temperature results in climate change

Human life depends on biodiversity

Statutory nuisance

Statutory nuisances are activities that might be prejudicial (damaging) to people's health or interfere with a person's legitimate use and enjoyment of his/her property – for example:

- emissions of smoke, gases and fumes

- dust

- steam and smells

- piles of rubbish

- animals

- noise.

Sustainability

Sustainability, in environmental terms, can be described as the ability to maintain human functions into the future. For humans to live sustainably, the Earth's resources must be used at a rate at which they can be replenished.

The World Commission on Environment and Development defines sustainability as development that 'meets the needs of the present without compromising the ability of future generations to meet their own needs'.

The concept of sustainability is complex and encompasses three key areas known as the 'three pillars', which are:

- the environment

- society

- economy.

Finding a balance where a community is financially viable, socially equitable and environmentally sustainable is the goal.

Personal social responsibility

As individuals, we are all responsible for the environment. This concept is known as personal social responsibility and expresses the ideal that everyone takes responsibility for his or her own actions. With regards to the environment, it is recognised that even apparently insignificant individual actions can lead to big changes.

Chapter 2
Understanding environmental aspects

Definitions

The term environmental aspect is defined as 'the elements of an organisation's activities, products or services that can interact with the environment' (source: ISO 14001: 2004).

Examples of environmental aspects include the:

■ use of resources (such as water or energy)

■ production of solid or hazardous waste

■ production of air emissions.

The term environmental impact is defined as 'any change to the environment, whether adverse or beneficial, wholly or partially resulting from an organisation's activities, products or services' (source: ISO 14001: 2004).

Examples of environmental impacts include:

- resource depletion
- air pollution
- climate change
- water pollution
- contaminated land
- loss of biodiversity
- statutory nuisances.

Identifying aspects and impacts

In order to identify the aspects and impacts of an organisation, you need to consider the following:

- inputs – the products, services and materials that go into the production of the organisation's output

- operations – what is involved in the manufacture of products or the delivery of services, and what materials and resources are used

- outputs – what is produced at the end of the process, both in terms of goods/services and waste products

- normal, abnormal and emergency situations – how aspects and impacts change as circumstances change

- indirect aspects and impacts – for example those of customers or the supply chain.

Monitoring

To control the risk of causing any adverse changes to the environment, it is important for organisations to measure and monitor environmental aspects and impacts.

By measuring environmental aspects and impacts, an organisation can check whether or not its controls are working.

A simple monitoring programme could involve:

- establishing the current state of environmental practice in the organisation
- prioritising measures depending on type of organisation and its specific environmental aspects and impacts
- measuring achievements
- benchmarking against industry or government best practice.

Business benefits

The legal, financial and moral benefits for organisations that incorporate environmental best practice include:

- compliance – reduced risk of prosecution, licence to operate may be based on environmental credentials

- cost savings – avoidance of legal costs and fines associated with prosecution, savings linked to forward planning and reduced energy and resources use and waste

- reduced impact on environment – contributing to sustainability and enhanced reputation (customers, staff, community and enforcement authorities), which in turn could impact on sales and business growth.

Chapter 3
Principles of environmental law

Key principles

There are four key principles that underpin all environmental laws:

- the polluter pays principle
- producer responsibilities – the duty of manufacturers to consider the environmental impacts of their products
- integrated pollution prevention and control (IPPC) – to ensure that pollution prevention in one area does not lead to pollution in another
- preventive approach, precautionary principle – it is always better to take precautions to prevent pollution than to deal with an environmental emergency.

Manufacturers have a duty to consider the environmental impact of their products

Environmental law in the UK is shaped by European and international law. There are environmental laws affecting:

- Air – covering emissions of gases, dark smoke and other airborne pollutants that harm the quality of the atmosphere. It includes environmental permitting and authorising regimes and, via the climate change framework, establishes financial incentives to switch to less-polluting ways of working.

- Land – covering nature conservation, pollution from agricultural operations, contaminated land (including radioactive contamination) and liability for environmental damage.

- Water – covering discharges to sewers, surface water and groundwater, water abstraction and impounding, and the protection of water against agricultural nitrate pollution.

Other areas of environmental law cover:

- use of chemicals
- energy
- environmental permitting
- noise and statutory nuisance
- pesticides and biocides
- radioactive substances
- waste.

International policy instruments

The role of international law is, through a system of agreements, to bring nations together to tackle common issues and concerns. A major force in international law is the United Nations. A number of key agreements enshrine international law and policy.

- The Kyoto Protocol is intended to achieve 'stabilization of greenhouse gas concentrations in the atmosphere at a level that would prevent dangerous anthropogenic interference with the climate system'.

- The Montreal Protocol is an international treaty designed to protect the ozone layer by phasing out the production of a number of substances believed to be responsible for ozone depletion.

- The Convention on International Trade in Endangered Species of Wild Fauna and Flora (CITES) aims to ensure that international trade in specimens of wild animals and plants does not threaten their survival and it accords varying degrees of protection to more than 33,000 species of animals and plants.

Regulators

There are two main regulatory bodies that implement and monitor environmental policy in the UK:

- The Environment Agency is the statutory environmental protection organisation in England and Wales. Its areas of responsibility include:

  – pollution control of industries, including chemical plants and power stations, which could cause major environmental damage

  – water resources and water quality

  – waste regulation

  – contaminated land and radioactive substances

  – flood defences

  – fisheries and navigation

  – water-related conservation and recreation.

The Scottish Environment Protection Agency (SEPA) has similar responsibilities in Scotland, as well as additional duties to control air pollution from a wide variety of organisations. In Northern Ireland, the main environmental regulator is the Northern Ireland Environment Agency (NIEA).

- Local authorities – regulation of the environment at local government level is in the hands of environmental health officers (EHOs) whose responsibilities include:

  - preventing air pollution from businesses not regulated by the environment agencies

  - taking action against other local environmental problems, such as dust and smells from industrial sites, litter and noise pollution (statutory nuisance).

Other organisations, such as local water companies and Natural England also have an impact.

Consequences of infringing environmental law

Inspectors from the environment agencies and EHOs from local authorities have powers to enforce environmental legislation. They can, for instance:

- visit and inspect the premises of an organisation at any time to ensure that it is complying with the law
- enforce compliance with the law and impose a schedule of works and timings, paid for by the polluting organisation
- stop an organisation from operating if there is thought to be a serious risk to the environment.

Legal penalties include:

- closure of business
- fines
- prison sentences
- payment of compensation
- clean-up costs (e.g. the polluter pays principle).

Enforcement officers
can inspect premises
at any time

Organisations that
pose a serious risk can
be shut down

Legal penalties
include fines

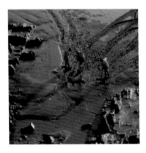

and clean-up costs

Regulations affecting pollution

Regulations covering air, land and water pollution include:

- **Integrated pollution prevention and control** (IPPC) – a regulatory system based on an integrated approach to control the environmental impact to air, land and water of emissions arising from industrial activities. It involves determining the appropriate controls for industry to protect the environment through a single permitting process.

- **Environmental permitting** – a regulatory system issuing permits for waste and pollution control. Other permitting regimes cover discharge consents, water abstraction and radioactive substance regulation.

- **Carbon reduction commitment** (CRC) incorporates regulations affecting the reduction of carbon emissions in large organisations (with output greater than 6,000 MWh) who must:

  - buy allowances

  - monitor, assess and manage emissions throughout the emissions year.

Ensuring legal compliance

There are a number of steps an organisation can take to ensure compliance, including:

- making a list of all relevant environmental law

- monitoring policy and legal developments to ensure that any changes are anticipated

- developing appropriate work procedures, based on current law and best practice guidelines, and training staff

- monitoring to ensure that such procedures are implemented in full.

Chapter 4
Energy use and carbon management

The greenhouse effect and global warming

The greenhouse effect is the process whereby solar radiation, reflected by the Earth's surface, is trapped by a number of 'greenhouse gases' in the atmosphere and warms the Earth. The process is called the greenhouse effect because it is thought that the gases retain the heat like the glass in a greenhouse.

Greenhouse gases trap heat from the sun

The greenhouse effect results in global warming

There are five main greenhouse gases (GHGs) in the atmosphere that trap heat from the sun and warm the Earth:

- carbon dioxide – released when fossil fuels are burned

- methane – released as a by-product of animal digestion

- nitrous oxide – released when fossil fuels are burned

- fluorinated hydrocarbons (hydroflurocarbons or HFCs) – released when refrigerants leak from air conditioning systems

- sulphur hexafluorides – released by leakage from electrical sub-stations.

Carbon dioxide is released when fossil fuels are burned

Methane is released as a by-product of animal digestion

Most of these gases are naturally occurring, and life is only possible on Earth because the atmosphere retains heat from the sun. However, human activities – in particular, the production of carbon dioxide from industrial production and pollution and methane from waste and animal husbandry – have led to conditions that have increased the 'greenhouse effect', which has, in turn, caused global warming and climate change.

Global warming is the average annual increase in global temperature.

The impacts of climate change

Climate change is the result of global warming and has different effects in different parts of the world, such as:

- a rise in the mean global temperature

- melting of the polar ice caps

- rising sea levels

- more frequent and extreme weather events, such as droughts and storms.

These effects could, in turn, cause:

- environmental damage, human injury, ill health and loss of life

- increased risk of flooding and rising sea defence costs

- land surface loss due to rising sea levels, resulting in population migration and infrastructure adaptation costs

- agricultural disruption, affecting food availability and increasing the gap between rich and poor

- increased risk of water- and food-borne diseases and the spread of tropical diseases

- loss of natural habitats (already occurring in certain ecosystems – for example coral reefs and polar ice caps).

Tackling climate change

Climate change is being tackled on a global scale by international laws and voluntary commitments to reduce consumption of carbon-based fossil fuels and, therefore, GHG emissions. For example:

- the Kyoto agreement introduced the concept of 'common but differentiated responsibilities' – the European Union has committed to an 8 per cent reduction by 2012 in GHG emissions compared to 1990 levels

- the European Union energy policy commits to a 20 per cent reduction in GHGs by 2020

- the EU Emissions Trading Scheme (ETS) introduced carbon trading, a legally binding framework that requires businesses in key sectors – such as energy, steel, cement, glass, brick making, and paper/cardboard manufacture – to buy carbon credits for the amount of carbon dioxide they emit

- England and Wales, under the Climate Change Act 2008, are committed to an 80 per cent reduction (against the 1990 baseline) in GHG emissions by 2050 and the introduction of corporate carbon reporting.

Carbon footprinting

A carbon footprint is 'the total set of GHG emissions caused directly and indirectly by an individual, organisation, event or product' (The Carbon Trust, 2008). Carbon footprints are measured by a GHG emissions assessment.

There are simple measures that can be taken to reduce energy consumption and, therefore, the carbon footprint of an organisation. These include:

Heating:

- insulate buildings to keep heat in
- close doors
- turn down heating rather than opening windows
- turn down heating in low occupancy areas
- service boilers regularly and consider central control of thermostat.

Lighting:

- turn off lights in areas not in use
- use low-energy light bulbs.

Equipment:

- turn off all equipment when not in use
- do not leave equipment on standby
- specify energy-efficient equipment.

Transport:

- reduce vehicle usage
- turn off engines when not in use
- plan routes in advance to increase journey efficiency
- accelerate/decelerate slowly (reducing fuel use by 15–30 per cent).

Choose products that
are recycled

or recyclable

Consider life cycle
costs, energy use and
carbon emissions

and how the product will
be disposed of at the end
of its life

Sustainable purchasing

Another way to reduce the carbon footprint and environmental impact of an organisation is to introduce a policy of sustainable purchasing – taking environmental and social factors into account in purchasing decisions. It is about looking at what products are made of, where they come from and who has made them.

The principles of sustainable purchasing can be incorporated into procurement regimes by:

- thoroughly assessing the need for the product or service to be purchased

- choosing products with recycled content or that are recyclable/ biodegradable and locally-produced

- considering life cycle cost, energy usage and carbon emissions of the product

- considering how the product will be disposed of at the end of its life

- choosing suppliers with credible policies relating to environmental management and corporate social responsibility and that comply with relevant environmental legislation.

Chapter 5

Resource efficiency and waste minimisation

Renewable and non-renewable resources

A renewable resource is a:

- natural resource that can be replaced by natural processes at a rate comparable or faster than its rate of consumption by humans – for example, water or oxygen

- commodity produced in a sustainable manner or recycled – for example timber or metal.

A non-renewable resource is a natural resource or commodity that cannot be produced, re-grown, regenerated or reused on a scale to sustain the rate of consumption – for example fossil fuels.

Life cycle assessment

Identifying the impact of each stage of a product's sourcing, manufacture, distribution, use and disposal is called life cycle assessment.

Waste regulations

Most UK legislation controlling waste management is implemented as a result of European directives. The EC Directive on Waste (75/442/EEC, as amended), better known as the Waste Framework Directive, establishes a framework for the management of waste across the European Union.

The legislation requires that anyone who treats, keeps, deposits or disposes of waste has a waste management permit (unless exempted or excluded).

A key objective of the permit system is to ensure that waste is recovered or disposed of without endangering human health and without using processes or methods that harm the environment.

Anyone who imports, produces, carries, keeps, treats or disposes of waste is subject to a duty of care, whereby they must take all reasonable and applicable measures to:

- prevent another person illegally treating, keeping, depositing or otherwise disposing of the waste

- prevent the escape of waste

- ensure that transfer of the waste only occurs to an 'authorised person' and that the transfer is accompanied by a written description of the waste.

Legislation also classifies waste by type – for example:

- controlled waste – including household, industrial and commercial waste not otherwise classified

- hazardous waste – containing properties harmful to human health or the environment (for example chemicals, batteries or clinical waste)

- waste electrical and electronic equipment (WEEE) – the by-products of electrical components such as computers, mobile phones or printers

- packaging – any materials used for the protection, delivery and presentation of goods, from the producer to the user.

Producers of commercial waste have a legal duty to ensure proper and appropriate disposal. They must prove that the waste is:

- segregated

- accurately described and classified

- stored

- secure

- transferred in authorised waste carriers

- disposed of at authorised sites.

Producer responsibility

'Producer responsibility' is an extension of the polluter pays principle aimed at ensuring that businesses that place products on the market take responsibility for those products once they have reached the end of their life.

In law, producer responsibility is imposed on the following types of waste:

- end-of-life vehicles
- waste electrical and electronic equipment (WEEE)
- batteries
- packaging and packaging waste.

Producer responsibilities
are imposed on
end-of-life vehicles

waste electrical and
electronic equipment

batteries

packaging and
packaging waste

Resource efficiency and waste minimisation

Resource inefficiency produces waste of various kinds, all of which have an impact on the environment – for example:

- landfill:
  - contaminates land
  - produces toxic leachates that pollute water courses
  - uses land
  - creates smell, dust and noise nuisance
  - releases methane, a greenhouse gas
- uncontrolled incineration releases atmospheric pollution
- atmospheric release:
  - discharges toxins with possible health implications
  - creates smog
  - damages buildings

- uncontrolled effluent discharge:

  - reduces drinking water quality

  - affects wildlife habitats

  - diminishes fish stocks

  - damages human health.

Resource efficiency requires selecting resources, products and services that use the minimum energy in their production or delivery and result in the least possible waste.

The benefits to business of resource efficiency and waste minimisation include reducing the costs of:

- purchasing

- processing (including energy consumption)

- waste disposal

- transportation.

The waste hierarchy

The waste hierarchy identifies waste disposal options and ranks them in order of increasing environmental impact. All organisations should aim to eliminate waste from the outset. If this is not practical or possible, organisations should consider reducing, reusing or recycling waste. If none of these measures can be applied, then organisations must dispose of waste in a responsible manner.

1. Eliminate

Avoid producing waste
in the first place

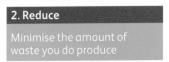

2. Reduce

Minimise the amount of
waste you do produce

3. Reuse

Use items as many times
as possible

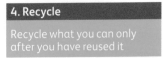

4. Recycle

Recycle what you can only
after you have reused it

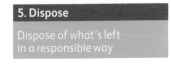

5. Dispose

Dispose of what's left
in a responsible way

The role of the consumer

The consumer can help drive environmental change by applying the principles of sustainable purchasing:

- buy only what is necessary
- consider the life cycle costs of the product from source to waste
- choose a product with minimal packaging
- ensure the product is energy efficient
- ensure the product is long lasting
- ensure the product is repairable
- choose a product made from renewable or sustainable sources
- take transportation costs and air miles into account
- buy a recycled and recyclable product.

Chapter 6
Water management

Managing water

As well as being essential for life, clean water has many industrial uses. It is vital that water is effectively managed to maintain supplies and to avoid pollution from the discharges of industrial processes.

Maintaining water supplies requires management of the abstraction process. Groundwater abstraction is the process of taking water from a source beneath the Earth's surface, either temporarily or permanently.

Increasing pressure of population growth has led to water resources being stretched, and regular near-drought conditions have led to hosepipe bans and concerns that water supplies could fall short of demand.

Regulations control the:

■ amount of water that can abstracted

■ quality of water used to supply public drinking water

■ points of abstraction.

Water sources are often polluted by the discharge of effluent and chemicals. The worst offenders are:

■ oil pollution, caused by:

   – oil industry activities

   – leaks from storage tanks

   – the use of lubricants.

■ industrial pollution, caused by:

   – industrial effluent released into rivers

   – the use of detergents

   – fire water run off.

■ agricultural pollution, caused by:

   – use of pesticides

   – use of chemical fertilisers

   – silage and slurry.

Water pollution regulations

Under water pollution legislation it is an offence to cause or knowingly permit any poisonous, noxious or polluting matter or solid waste to enter controlled waters without a discharge consent (other defences are permissible).

In order to obtain a discharge consent, an organisation must apply to the Environment Agency and:

- demonstrate knowledge of what is being discharged and where it is going
- provide evidence that discharges are regularly monitored
- not de-water directly into a watercourse without prior consent.

Another key piece of water pollution legislation relates to oil storage requirements, which requires that storage vessels have secondary containment, to ensure that oil does not leak into the environment should the first container fail. The containment or bund should be:

- of an appropriate size (110 per cent volume)
- in an appropriate location away from any controlled waters
- protected from damage.

Water management

Water is used in every organisation. Simple water management starts with understanding how much operations and appliances use.

Effectively managing water involves:

- reducing water use

- reusing water

- selecting equipment that economises on water use

- maintaining plumbing to prevent water loss through dripping taps and leaks.

The twelve most water-intensive domestic operations and appliances have been labelled the 'dirty dozen'. These are, in order (the most water intensive first):

- bath (average volume)
- washing machine (per cycle)
- dishwasher (average cycle)
- power shower (per minute)
- washing up (per session)
- hosepipe (per minute)
- pressure washer (per minute)
- shower (per minute)
- toilet (per flush)
- running tap (per minute)
- watering can (average volume)
- dripping tap (per minute).

Chapter 7
Pollution prevention and emergency planning

Emergency situations

However effective anti-pollution measures are, there will always be potential for accidents.

A pollution emergency can occur in just about any location. Serious incidents can result in the contamination of air, water or land.

Such emergencies have both direct and indirect consequences for humans and the environment and can lead to:

- risk to human health and life
- destruction of ecosystems
- destruction of property
- costs of cleaning up
- costs to insurers
- loss of business.

Source, pathway, receptor

Environmental risk management systems break down potential pollution incidents into three parts:

- source – the point of release or where the pollution originates

- pathway – the part of the environment through which the pollution moves

- receptor – what is affected by the pollution – human health or wildlife, for instance.

Identifying the source, pathway and receptor can helps us to assess the risks – and, thereby, ensure that appropriate controls are in place to minimise the effects – of a potential pollution incident.

Emergency planning, training and resources

Preventing the worst effects of a pollution incident requires planning, training and resources.

In most cases, the effects of such incidents can be controlled, providing appropriate pollution prevention procedures are in place. The key is to have in place a contingency, or pollution incident response, plan.

The level of response will depend on health and safety issues, staff training, the level of personal protective equipment (PPE) available, the nature of any spilled materials and the types of pollution control equipment available on the site.

When the risks are high – as, for instance, with oil spills – regulations are in place to control the reporting of and response to an emergency.

For other types of incidents, a checklist of actions can be useful and should typically address the following issues:

- fire-fighting strategy

- alerting nearby properties, downstream abstractors or environmentally sensitive sites that could be affected

- procedures for alerting staff on site and, where appropriate, adjacent sites, including evacuation procedures

- contacting the emergency services, relevant agency or local authority

- substances posing particular risks

- the selection of the appropriate level of PPE

- making leaking containers safe

- procedures for containing leaks, spills and fire-fighting run-off

- procedures for the recovery of spilled product and the safe handling and legal disposal of any wastes arising.

Preparations for an emergency should also include:

- inspection regimes to ensure that if there are problems with equipment that might lead to an emergency, they are spotted quickly

- early detection systems where appropriate to prevent leaks becoming too serious

- procedures for physical containment using pollution control equipment, such as bunds to soak up spillages

- provision of emergency equipment such as spill kits and PPE

- training of staff so that they know exactly what is required in the event of an emergency.

In the event of an oil leak or spill, the recommended course of action is to:

- STOP it at the source and use absorbing material such as sand

- CONTAIN the oil to prevent it entering any drains or watercourses

- CALL the Environment Agency.

Reporting

Pollution incidents must be reported to the relevant authorities so that effective steps can be taken to clean up the pollution and any residual problems that might lead to further incidents can be identified and controlled.

Chapter 8
Environmental management systems

An environmental management system (EMS) is a structured framework for managing an organisation's significant environmental impacts.

A number of stages are involved in the implementation of an effective EMS:

- commitment from the top management is required to ensure that the resources and the will to create an EMS are present

- environmental review – this involves analysis of the current state of the organisation's environmental management system, environmental aspects (elements of the organisation's activities, products and services that could have an impact on the environment) and legal and other requirements

- policy – top management must define the environmental policy (in line with the requirements of ISO 14001), which must be communicated to all staff working for and on behalf of the organisation and must be made available to all interested parties

- planning – staff responsible for each stage of implementation should be selected, resources allocated and objectives, targets and action plans set – a plan of improvement should be developed for some significant environmental aspects

- implementation and operation – training and supervision is required to implement the plan throughout the organisation

- monitoring and auditing – environmental performance indicators should be used to track changes and a regular audit is required to monitor the systems and their effectiveness

- review – regular reviews at management level ensure that improvements are made where necessary.

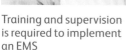

Training and supervision is required to implement an EMS

Benefits to the organisation

An EMS can help:

- provide a structured and proportionate approach to environmental issues

- advanced planning and resource management, which can lead to cost savings

- legal compliance – an EMS is a legal requirement for organisations that fall within the integrated pollution prevention and control (IPPC) regime

- management of environmental resources and provide access to investment, new markets and increased sales

- reduce environmental impacts, resulting in better relations with staff, community and regulators.

Environmental policy

An environmental policy provides the context, strategy, commitment and direction for an EMS.

The policy must be communicated to all staff working for and on behalf of the organisation and must be made available to all interested parties. This policy must state the organisation's commitment to:

- pollution prevention
- legal compliance
- continual improvement.

Environmental action plan

An environmental action plan puts an environmental policy into practice. It outlines responsibilities, activities and timing. Typically, an environmental action plan will:

- list key goals and provide the means for achieving them

- be based on SMART (specific, measurable, achievable, responsibility assigned and time bound) objectives.

An organisation's commitment to pollution prevention can take many forms

Engagement

A key issue in the fight to protect the environment is engagement. Persuading people of the importance of environmental issues and convincing them that individual and collective action can make a difference is one of the biggest challenges faced by government, environment agencies and organisations.

There are many ways of engaging interest in environmental issues, including:

■ education

■ providing help and information

■ peer pressure.